Wonders of the Webb Telescope

Our Solar System

Mari Bolte

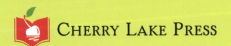

Published in the United States of America by Cherry Lake Publishing Group
Ann Arbor, Michigan
www.cherrylakepublishing.com

Reading Adviser: Beth Walker Gambro, MS, Ed., Reading Consultant, Yorkville, IL
Content Adviser: Robert S. Kowalczyk, MS, Physics, Systems Engineer (Retired) at the NASA Jet Propulsion Laboratory

Photo Credits: page 1: ©Jose A. Bernat Bacete/Getty Images; page 1: ©NASA, ESA, CSA, Jupiter ERS Team; image processing by Judy Schmidt/nasa.gov; page 5: ©Yuga Kurita/Getty Images; page 6: ©Vadim Sadovski/Shutterstock; page 9: ©Beyond Space/Shutterstock; page 10: ©Webb NIRCam composite image (two filters) of Jupiter system, unlabeled (top) and labeled (bottom). Credit: NASA, ESA, CSA, Jupiter ERS Team; image processing by Ricardo Hueso (UPV/EHU) and Judy Schmidt./flickr.com; page 12: ©Lockheed Martin/flickr.com; page 15: ©NASA/JPL-Caltech/nasa.gov; page 16: ©NASA, ESA, CSA, W.M. Keck Observatory, A. Pagan (STScI), JWST Titan GTO Team./flickr.com; page 19: ©Pavel Gabzdyl/Shutterstock; page 20: ©NASA, ESA, CSA, STScI/flickr.com; page 23: ©Jcpag2012/NASA/Wikimedia; page 23: ©Luc Viatour/Wikimedia; page 23: ©ESA/ATG medialab/esa.int; page 25: ©24K-Production/Getty Images; page 26: ©Arianespace, ESA, NASA, CSA, CNES/flickr.com; page 28: ©Northrop Grumman /nasa.gov; page 30: ©Halfpoint Images/Getty Images

Copyright © 2024 by Cherry Lake Publishing Group

All rights reserved. No part of this book may be reproduced or utilized in any form or by any means without written permission from the publisher.

Cherry Lake Press is an imprint of Cherry Lake Publishing Group.

Library of Congress Cataloging-in-Publication Data
Cataloging-in-Publication Data has been filed and is available at catalog.loc.gov.

ISBN 9781668938379 Lib.

Cherry Lake Publishing Group would like to acknowledge the work of the Partnership for 21st Century Learning, a Network of Battelle for Kids. Please visit Battelle for Kids online for more information.

Note from publisher: Websites change regularly, and their future contents are outside of our control. Supervise children when conducting any recommended online searches for extended learning opportunities.

Printed in the United States of America

Mari Bolte is an author and editor of children's books in every subject imaginable. She hopes the next generation sets their sights on the sky and beyond. Never stop the love of learning!

CONTENTS

Chapter 1
In the Beginning | 4

Chapter 2
Jupiter in a New Light | 8

Chapter 3
A Titanic View | 14

Chapter 4
Put a Ring on It | 18

Chapter 5
Humanity's Last Glimpse of the James Webb Space Telescope | 24

Activity | 30
Find Out More | 31
Glossary | 32
Index | 32

CHAPTER 1

In the Beginning

The first space telescope was launched in 1962. Its mission was to study the Sun. Four years later, the *Orbiting Astronomical Observatory* followed. It would study cosmic objects outside Earth's atmosphere. But scientists dreamed bigger. They began building a new telescope. It would show them the entire **solar system**. In 1990, the *Hubble Space Telescope* was sent into space. It is still orbiting Earth today.

Our solar system is around 4.5 billion years old. It is constantly changing, moving, and growing. Outside of our solar system, stars are born. Then they die. Galaxies collide. There are undiscovered planets that might support life. *Hubble* showed us the first glimpses of these never-before-seen things. So far, it has taken more than a million images of objects in the sky.

Telescopes on Earth have been aimed at the sky since the 1600s.

Even before *Hubble* launched, though, "What's next?" was already being asked. *Hubble* would watch the universe from above our planet. The scientists wanted the next telescope to go even farther. It would see farther, be more powerful, and show us even more. On December 25, 2021, the *James Webb Space Telescope* left Earth. By January 24, it reached its final destination. It was nearly 1 million miles (1.6 million kilometers) from our planet.

Large telescope mirrors can COLLECT MORE LIGHT and do it faster. Objects with less light or that are farther away show up better with these mirrors.

Telescope Facts

This image combines separate images of *Hubble* and *Webb*. The two telescopes have never been photographed together.

The *WEBB TELESCOPE* is 100 times more sensitive to light than *Hubble*.

Hubble (left) has a mirror that is 7.8 feet (2.4 meters) across. *Webb's* PRIMARY MIRROR is 21.7 feet (6.6 m) across. *Webb's* mirror is six times more powerful than *Hubble's* mirror.

CHAPTER 2

Jupiter in a New Light

Jupiter was first observed in detail back in 1610. Galileo Galilei saw it through a telescope. Cold clouds swirl across its surface. Past photos of Jupiter make it look like a sandy or orange-striped sphere. Then in August 2022, *Webb* gave the planet a new look.

Webb's mission is to study every stage of our universe's history. The National Aeronautics and Space Administration (NASA) shared the telescope's first image on July 11, 2022. *Webb* uses three different cameras. Each picture it takes combines dozens, hundreds, or even thousands of shots taken over a period of hours. Things that are millions of **light-years** away are bright and full of detail. Things hidden in clouds of **space dust** are suddenly clear. And even familiar things are seen in a new light—literally.

This artist's representation shows Jupiter, the largest planet in our solar system.

The image *Webb* sent back (on the following pages) was able to pick up Jupiter's rings. They are a million times fainter than the planet itself. Two of the planet's satellites, or moons, can be seen as well. One is touching the ring that circles the planet's center. The other is brighter and directly to the left. In the lower part of the image, far-off galaxies look like small blurs.

The bright spots in the image are reflecting the SUN'S LIGHT. They are clouds at higher altitudes than the planet's other gases.

Jupiter's two moons that are visible to the left of its rings are called AMALTHEA and ADRASTEA.

Amalthea →   Adrastea →

Jupiter's famous GREAT RED SPOT shows up as white light under Webb's infrared filters. Scientists believe the brightness is from high-**altitude** hazes that float above the clouds. The darker spots on the planet have less cloud cover.

Jupiter Facts

A scientist inspects the NIRCam in this image from 2014, 7 years before *Webb* was launched.

Two of *Webb*'s cameras use near-**infrared** light. The Near-Infrared Camera (NIRCam) can capture images in high definition. The Near InfraRed **Spectrograph** (NIRSpec) can observe more than 100 objects in space at the same time.

The Near Infrared Imager and Slitless Spectrograph (NIRISS) takes the highest-resolution images of bright objects.

The third camera is the Mid-Infrared Instrument (MIRI). It detects mid-infrared light from galaxies that are very far away. Their spectrum has shifted to mid-infrared due to the expansion of the universe.

When *Webb*'s images are first sent back to Earth, they look nearly black. But that's because human eyes, and even computer screens, can't process the different shades of gray in them. The images are tweaked and combined. Textures, shadows, and highlighted areas show up. Finally, special processors turn the infrared light into light people are able to see. This is how *Webb*'s images of Jupiter were made.

MEET THE TEAM

The *James Webb Space Telescope* didn't build itself! NASA headed the project. The European Space Agency (ESA) and the Canadian Space Agency (CSA) collaborated. More than 1,200 scientists, engineers, and technicians worked together to make it happen. They designed and built parts in 14 different countries and 27 states. The project's longest employee was Charlie Atkinson. He signed onto the project in 1998. Today, he is the chief engineer.

Construction began in 2004. Pieces were created and tested. Then they went to NASA's Goddard Space Flight Center in Maryland. All 18 of *Webb*'s mirrors were installed in 2015. The final steps to completion began in 2019.

CHAPTER 3

A Titanic View

Saturn is the sixth planet in our solar system. It is the second-largest overall. It is surrounded by 124 moons. Some are tiny, around the size of a sports arena. Others are enormous. Titan is the largest. It is about 40 percent of Earth's size. That's larger than the planet Mercury!

In 2005, the *Cassini* spacecraft entered Saturn's orbit. The *Huygens* probe had hitched a ride aboard the spacecraft. It dropped off *Cassini* and parachuted down to Titan's surface. It took the first-ever photos of the moon. But Titan's dense clouds remained a mystery.

Webb's infrared camera built on the *Huygens* probe's work. *Webb* can see through the clouds. It showed Titan's light and dark patches. It showed scientists where clouds developed. *Webb*'s photos were compared to pictures from

Cassini spent 20 years in space. Thirteen of them were spent in Saturn's orbit, as seen in this still from a computer-animated film made by NASA.

the Keck telescope in Hawaii taken 2 days later. The clouds seemed to be in the same place—but they had changed shape. The scientists were excited. Clouds don't last long on Titan. That makes them hard to study. Being able to see them from two different telescopes gave the scientists a clearer picture of the cloudy moon.

This image shows *WEBB'S FIRST LOOK* at Titan. The gases that surround the planet give it a fuzzy look.

Webb NIRCam, November 4, 2022

Titan Facts

In the past, scientists were able to capture high-resolution images of about 9 percent of Titan's surface. Another 25 TO 30 PERCENT was captured in lower resolution. An **algorithm** was used to fill in the image gaps.

Keck NIRC-2, November 6, 2022

Earth and Titan are the only planetary bodies in our solar system with rivers, lakes, and seas. Earth's are made of water. Titan's are made of LIQUIFIED GAS!

17

CHAPTER 4

Put a Ring on It

Neptune is the farthest-away planet in our solar system. It was first discovered in 1846. Saturn's rings were first seen in the 1600s through a telescope on Earth. Jupiter's and Uranus's rings were seen in the late 1970s. For many years, scientists wondered if Neptune was surrounded by rings as well. It seemed to make sense that it would have them. In 1984, scientists watched as the planet passed in front of a distant star. There were extra blinks before and after the overlap. This seemed to be extra proof that there could be rings.

It would be another 5 years before they could prove it once and for all, though. On August 22, 1989, the spacecraft *Voyager 2* passed by. It took the first pictures of Neptune's rings. A decade later, *Hubble* took more images. This time, Neptune's rings were shown in detail.

French astronomer and mathematician Urbain Le Verrier discovered Neptune, shown here as a 3D illustration.

Neptune has five main rings made up of small rocks and space dust. The rings are not even all the way around. They are also relatively new. Scientists found that they are much younger than the solar system. It's possible that one of Neptune's moons got too close. The planet's gravity tore it apart.

Neptune Facts

Neptune's five rings are named ADAMS, ARAGO, GALLE, LASSELL, and LE VERRIER. They were named after astronomers who studied the planet.

The THIN BANDS OF DUST around Neptune had never been seen before in infrared.

The planet has 14 MOONS. Two can be seen to the right of the planet. Look closely around the rings to see the others!

In regular images, Neptune looks blue. But NIRCam uses near-infrared waves. The planet's methane gas absorbs infrared light. This gives *Webb*'s photo (on pgs. 20–21) a darker look. The lighter places are high-altitude clouds made of methane and ice. They reflect sunlight before the surface methane absorbs it.

There is a bright line around the middle of the planet. Scientists believe this is caused by global atmospheric circulation. These are wind systems that move hot air to cooler **poles**. The warmer air looks like it's glowing under near-infrared.

Huge spinning storms have been seen on Neptune. *Voyager 2* first spotted a high-powered storm in 1989. Scientists called the gathered storm clouds the Great Dark Spot. This storm was larger than Earth.

When the *Hubble Space Telescope* looked again in 1994, the Great Dark Spot was gone. In its place was a different dark spot. *Webb*'s image showed a similar storm to the south of the planet. Like the glowing clouds, the spot shows up as bright rather than dark.

The north pole of the planet can't be seen in *Webb's* image. This is because of where Neptune is in its orbit. However, that area looks bright as well. It could be a hint that clouds and storms are building.

Where's Webb?

The *James Webb* is 1 million miles (1.6 million km) away from Earth. It is orbiting the Sun at the second Lagrangian point. This point is directly behind Earth as viewed from the Sun. Being there keeps the telescope in line with Earth as the planet orbits the Sun.

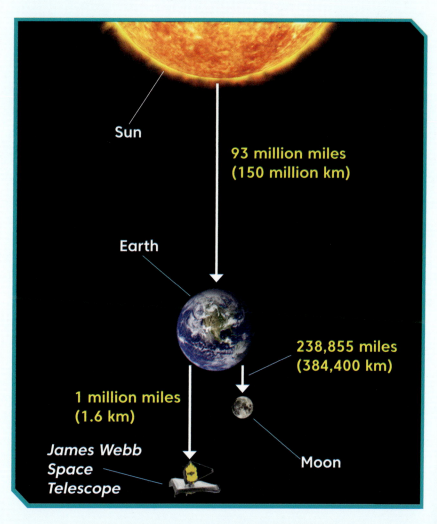

CHAPTER 5

Humanity's Last Glimpse of the *James Webb Space Telescope*

Webb left Earth on December 25, 2021. It was safely tucked inside an *Ariane 5* rocket. They are among the safest and most reliable rockets ever made. The rocket launched from Europe's Spaceport in French Guiana. Launching near the equator gives rockets a boost with the energy from Earth's rotation. Earth's surface moves at 1,038 miles (1,670 km) per hour at the equator. At the poles, it moves at only 0.00005 miles (0.00008 km) per hour.

Scientists communicate with *Webb*, seen here in an artist's representation, constantly. It takes about 5 seconds for information from *Webb* to reach Earth.

After the rocket reached outer space, it began its 29-day journey to the second Lagrangian point. It had been tucked up inside the rocket's hull. Once they separated, it began unfolding. By day 14, it was fully reassembled.

Webb Facts

The last view of *Webb* before it headed into deep space was taken on December 26. It was taken by cameras on board the ARIANE ROCKET. Earth spans across the upper right of the photo.

Webb's **solar array** began deployment just 69 SECONDS after separating from *Ariane*. The solar array captures sunlight to power the telescope's tools.

Webb performed three planned CORRECTION BURNS during its trip. These bursts of energy kept the telescope on course so it would stop exactly where it was supposed to.

Webb can observe almost any point in the sky. At any one moment, around 39 percent of the sky can be seen in a single view. However, it can't see objects near Earth. The telescope's instruments must be kept cool at all times. Most of the cameras work best at −389 degrees Fahrenheit (−234 degrees Celsius).

The Sun gives off light and heat. The planets reflect the Sun's **radiation** and give off low levels of their own heat. A five-layer sunshield shades *Webb* while it works. However, the sunshield's position means the inside of our solar system is always out of view. If *Webb* was pointed at Earth or the Moon, the cameras would stop working. It would be like staring directly into the Sun. The brightness from Earth would also destroy the sensors.

Webb is too far away to repair or refuel. It was designed to complete a 5-year mission. Ten years of service is a target goal. It could even work for 20 years. That's into the 2040s! However, damage from space objects or instruments breaking could shorten that time. It is also too far away to bring home. The last photo taken by the *Ariane* rocket was the last time all of *Webb* will ever be seen with human eyes.

WHO WAS JAMES WEBB?

NASA was founded back in 1958. President Dwight D. Eisenhower signed it into existence. His successor, John F. Kennedy, committed to sending people to the Moon before the end of the 1960s. James Webb was put in charge of the young organization in 1961. He had worked in Washington, D.C., as a congressional aid. Then he went to law school. He served in the Marine Corps before and during World War II (1939–1945).

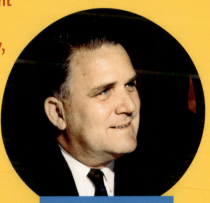

James E. Webb

Webb was not a scientist. But the job would be about policy, not about science. And he had proven that he could manage both people and money well.

Webb believed in Kennedy's goal, but he also wanted NASA to be scientific. NASA's contributions could help make aerospace engineering stronger. He vowed it would be more than a mission to send people to the Moon.

Under Webb's leadership, scientists were given more freedom. NASA improved its robotics program. They made spacecraft that could explore the Moon before people stepped foot on it. Probes flew past Mars and Venus, giving Americans their first look at outer space. By Webb's retirement in 1969, NASA had completed more than 75 missions to space.

Activity

Connect to STEAM: Science

More than 17,000 people work for NASA. Although not everyone is a scientist, there are 15 different types of scientists who work there. They do a variety of jobs, from designing instruments to managing projects. Some are experts in rocks. Others learn about plants or chemicals.

Find a scientist whose job sounds interesting. Visit NASA's career page with an adult. Read the stories from scientists there. Find out more about what they do. Then write the scientist a letter. Do you find them inspiring? Do you think their job is cool? Do you want to know how to get into their field?

If you want to send your letter, find out where your scientist works. Then use the internet to find the address. See if they write back!

Find Out More

Books

Bolte, Mari. *Journey to Mars*. Ann Arbor, MI: Cherry Lake Publishing, 2022.

Bradley, Doug. *Scientist*. New York: PowerKids Press, 2023.

Schaefer, Lola M. *Explore Rockets*. Minneapolis: Lerner Publications, 2023.

Thomas, Mindy. *Wow in Space: A Galactic Guide to the Universe and Beyond*. New York: Clarion Books, 2023.

Online Resources to Search with an Adult

Ariane Group: Find Out about the Launch of the *James Webb Space Telescope*

James Webb Space Telescope

Submit a Question to NASA

Webb Telescope: Quick Facts

Glossary

algorithm (AL-guh-rith-um) a set of instructions for solving a problem or accomplishing a task

altitude (AL-ti-tood) the height of an object above sea level or ground level

infrared (in-fruh-RED) invisible light from beyond the red end of the visible light spectrum

light-years (LITE-YEERZ) units of distance equal to how far light travels in 1 year—6 trillion miles (9.6 trillion km)

observatory (ub-ZUR-vuh-tor-ee) a place used for watching outer space

poles (POHLS) the two ends of an invisible axis that a planet rotates around; the farthest points from a planet's equator

radiation (ray-dee-AY-shuhn) energy that comes from a source in the form of waves or rays you cannot see

solar array (SOH-luhr uh-RAY) a solar panel that converts sunlight into electricity

solar system (SOH-lur SISS-tuhm) a sun and the objects in space that orbit around it

space dust (SPAYS DUHST) tiny bits of matter from comets, asteroids, and other space objects that collect into clouds

spectrograph (SPEK-troh-graf) a tool that breaks light down into bands of color

Index

Ariane 5 rockets, 24–28

Canadian Space Agency, 13
Cassini, 14

European Space Agency, 13

Galilei, Galileo, 8
Great Dark Spot, 22

Hubble Space Telescope, 4–5, 7, 18, 22
Huygens probe, 14

James Webb Space Telescope, 5–10, 12–14, 16, 22–24, 26–29
Jupiter, 8–11, 13, 18

Keck telescope, 15

mirrors, 6–7, 13
moons, 9–10, 14, 19, 21

NASA, 8, 13, 29
Neptune, 18–22

Orbiting Astronomical Observatory, 4

poles, 22, 24

rings, 9, 18–19, 21

Saturn, 14–15, 18
space dust, 8, 19, 21
sunshield, 28

Titan, 14–17

Voyager 2, 18, 22

Webb, James, 29